Original title:
Tassels on the Wind

Copyright © 2025 Creative Arts Management OÜ
All rights reserved.

Author: Elias Montgomery
ISBN HARDBACK: 978-1-80586-063-1
ISBN PAPERBACK: 978-1-80586-535-3

The Art of Letting Go

The fluff of fate is blowing free,
A dance of chaos, just you see!
With giggles caught in breezy flights,
Who knew the sky could wear such tights?

They twirl and twist like silly sprites,
Tickling clouds with their goofy sights!
A game of catch with gusts so bold,
They share their tales, but none are told.

Fragments of Airborne Beauty

In the park, they launch and sway,
Like bright confetti on a play day.
With shrieks of laughter hitting high,
As they spin freely through the sky.

A parade of colors, what a show!
With every gust, they steal the glow.
Chasing sunshine with a comic flair,
Oh, the joy that dances in the air!

Ripples of Color in the Sky

Look up now, can you see them there?
Spilling joy like they don't care!
A swirl of shades on breeze's breath,
As if they laugh at time and death.

The hues unite in playful spins,
Chasing each other, where fun begins!
With cheeky flaps and flutters so bright,
Who knew that soft things could take flight?

Dances of Delicate Appendages

A flurry of odd, untamed delight,
They pirouette in morning light.
With whispers bold and winks of cheer,
Innuendos tickle, but none can hear!

They frolic and flop with utmost glee,
Enticing giggles from you and me.
In this circus of colors, come join the show,
Where silliness reigns, with breezes in tow.

Fabrics of Spirit and Desire

In the closet, clothes so bold,
They dance around, if truth be told.
A shirt flips from side to side,
Waging laughter with each slide.

Ties wiggle like worms on a spree,
Belt loops shout, "Come laugh with me!"
A sweater's itch becomes a joke,
While socks conspire, a playful poke.

Floating Longing on the Horizon

A scarf takes flight on a morning breeze,
Flapping wildly, doing as it pleases.
A jacket pops out, ready to play,
Saying, "Catch me, I'll dance away!"

The sunbeams giggle, casting a glow,
On shorts that shout, "Let's steal the show!"
Flip-flops skitter, a tap-tap-tap,
As fashion joins in on this sunny wrap.

Elegance Embellished by Nature

A flowered dress spins with grace,
While bees buzz in a stylish race.
Leaves chuckle as they tumble down,
Joining the antics of a leafy gown.

Breezy hats tip their crowns in jest,
As nature plays host to the best-dressed.
A quick twirl sends petals in flight,
With laughter echoing through the daylight.

A Symphony of Free-flowing Embers

The curtains sway like dancers on cue,
While sunlight bows, proud and true.
A quilted throw joins the parade,
In a floral gala under shade.

Pillows leap, sprightly and bright,
Whispering secrets in the night.
Blankets giggle, fluffing their seams,
Stitching together our daydreams.

Adorned Ribbons at Twilight

In the breeze, they flail and dance,
A silly sight, they take a chance.
Draped on trees like party hats,
Swaying wildly – oh, the spats!

Neighbors chuckle, kids all cheer,
Who needs dogs when ribbons steer?
Twisting 'round like carefree fools,
Riding high, breaking all the rules.

Caress of Fabric in Flight

A silly scarf escapes the hand,
It spirals off to foreign land.
Like a kite, it sails the skies,
But oh! How it flops and flies.

Chasing after, feet all tangled,
Ribbons wrapping, legs get mangled.
With every gust, it sways and twirls,
Oh, the laughter as it whirls!

Breezy Collaborations

A curtain leaps from window's grip,
Joining in on nature's trip.
Swirling round like they're in tune,
As if they're dancing with the moon.

Hats take flight and wigs take wing,
Who knew fabric could so swing?
With a laugh, they twine and loop,
Making mischief, what a group!

Faded Colors on the Horizon

At twilight's end, the colors blend,
With ribbons frayed, they twist and bend.
Caught in laughter, fading fast,
Witty whispers of the past.

Sashes tripping on the ground,
An absurd comedy unbound.
As hues unite in sunset's glow,
The fabric giggles; off they go!

Streamers of Serenity

In the breeze they dance and swirl,
A rainbow twist of joy unfurl.
Chasing cats, they set the pace,
While squirrels plot a grand disgrace.

Up high they wave, then dive away,
Each flutter sings, it's time to play.
They tickle noses, tease the bees,
And kiss the cheeks of gentle trees.

The Gentle Lift of Deception

A gust arrives, and off they zoom,
Like cheeky sprites with mischief's bloom.
They hide behind the fence below,
And giggle soft, 'Look at them go!'

Unseen hands pull them to and fro,
As we all laugh, no need to know.
They taunt the hats of folks around,
And twist the words that dance to sound.

Threads of the Afternoon

Beneath the sun's delightful rays,
They flutter bright in playful ways.
A tapestry of laughter sewn,
With every lift, more joy is grown.

They tangle up with clouds above,
Inpiriting both joy and love.
A picnic spreads, the snacks run free,
While streamers weave a jubilee.

Frayed Ends in the Gales

The fabric flaps like wings of kin,
Inviting all to join the spin.
With every tug and playful jerk,
They leave behind a chuckling smirk.

Each gust reveals a cheeky twist,
A game of hide-and-seek, they insist.
Though some may rip and lose their charm,
They still spread cheer with every arm.

Cascading Moments of Grace

A dance upon the breeze, so light,
With socks that clash and colors bright.
They twirl in laughter, not a care,
As if they're flaunting what they wear.

A sudden gust, a sock takes flight,
It flaps and flutters, oh what a sight!
The neighbors giggle, children cheer,
As mismatched dreams drift far and near.

Whispering Colorstrands

In gardens filled with shades so bold,
The flowers gossip, tales unfold.
They chuckle softly, 'Look at me,'
A daisy's charm, a bumblebee.

With every flutter, petals sway,
They share secrets of the day.
A laugh escapes the tulips near,
Their colors brightening the atmosphere.

The Floating Symphony

A kite crewed by a crew of leaves,
Plays music with a rustling weave.
The sky applauds their aerial dance,
While squirrels watch with sideways glance.

In harmony, the breezes play,
While clouds become the stage each day.
Balloons inflate with giggling glee,
As laughter joins their symphony.

Aspirations in the Air

Balloons that dream of reaching heights,
While swaying in the sunny lights.
A wish floats by, a silly grin,
A dance of hopes where dreams begin.

The paper planes, they dive and glide,
With whispered dreams they cannot hide.
In every gust, a chuckle stirs,
As aspirations twist with furs.

Dappled Colors in the Sky's Embrace

In a world where kites do twirl,
A purple bird starts to whirl.
It drags along a tattered sock,
As giggles echo 'round the block.

The sun paints smiles upon the grass,
While squirrels dance like they have sass.
There's a cat that thinks it can fly,
But lands instead with a piteous sigh.

Lollipops attached to every breeze,
Tickling noses like honeyed bees.
The clouds do join in on the jest,
With fluffy puffs that never rest.

A rainbow's bend is quite the sight,
With crayons twinkling in broad daylight.
Oh, what a scene! Oh, what a hoot!
Nature's palette, so very astute!

Secrets Unfurled on Gentle Currents

Floating whispers in the air,
An umbrella's dared to take a dare.
With every gust, it's on a spree,
Chasing after a bumblebee.

A fish in a top hat swims by,
Winking as it gulps a pie.
Giggling leaves are in a chase,
Falling flat with a sideways grace.

The trees gossip with swaying trunks,
While mushrooms groove in colorful punks.
A ribbon curls in laughter's flight,
An unexpected twirl in the twilight.

Backyard secrets weave and spin,
While chickens dance with a cheeky grin.
In the meadow, absurdities bloom,
As the breeze carries joy in full plume.

Fanciful Flights of Color

Checkered balloons spill laughter wide,
While rainbows race in a zany glide.
Cupcakes dangle from a kite's arc,
As sprinklers giggle in the park.

A walrus wears oversized shades,
Strutting along where sunshine parades.
Ice cream drips on a joyful nose,
While the bunny burps and deeply glows.

Kaleidoscopic dreams take flight,
As ribbons whirl in sheer delight.
The sky erupts in confetti cheers,
With winks and nudges throughout the years.

Cactus strums a silly tune,
To a swooping hawk beneath the moon.
Every glance brings a chuckle near,
In this dreamland where joy draws near.

Yarned Memories in the Air

A yarn ball rolls with giggly cheer,
Tangled thoughts dance, oh-so-near.
Cats plot plots of tangled jobs,
While dogs just yawn with sleepy sobs.

Riding on a paper boat,
A thousand dreams that bumble and float.
A turtle dons a flashy hat,
While the goldfish winks, "Imagine that!"

Socks launch into the friendly sky,
In a contest to see who flies high.
The breeze weaves tales of silly fun,
With laughter echoing like a sun.

Kites tied to dreams skip along,
As wind carries a naughty song.
In this swirl where memories twine,
Funny moments happily align.

Twined Energies in the Wind

In the park, a floppy hat,
Flies away, what a chat!
Chasing squirrels, oh what fun,
Hats and tails, all on the run.

Breezy shoes take off their laces,
Dancing through the sunny spaces.
Umbrellas flip and take to flight,
A game of hide, a comic sight.

Pants trying to dance, oh dear!
Socks jump up and disappear.
Who needs kites when there's this show?
All our things want to say hello!

With laughter drifting high above,
Each item winks, how sweet the love!
For even in the careless play,
Life's a joke that whirls away.

Glorious Moving Patterns

Streamers hang and swirl around,
Laughter bubbling with each sound.
A paper airplane's sudden dive,
Is a testament of our jive.

Flying past the trees so green,
A tumble, oops! Quite unforeseen!
Dancers twirl, their ribbons flare,
Twisting, turning through the air.

A bee, a hat, a kite unite,
All colliding, what a sight!
We giggle as they intertwine,
Nature's chaos is divine.

Our picnic blanket starts to soar,
Hot dogs giggle, let's eat more!
With joyous gusts and chuckles grand,
Life's a play, so well planned.

Echoing Threads of Elysium

A jester's cap spins round and round,
Twirling tales just like a sound.
A classic whoopee cushion's cheer,
Makes the serious rats disappear.

With a flip, a flop, a laugh out loud,
The playful wind, it draws a crowd.
Each item's spirit floats along,
In a symphony, where all belong.

Puppies chase their puffy tails,
Dandelions whisper funny tales.
A bagpipe sings a wacky tune,
As bubbles burst, our jokes balloon.

Life's a circus full of jest,
In the breeze, we are all blessed.
So join the dance, the playful spin,
On this ride, let the fun begin!

Whims of the Sun-Kissed Air

Socks parade on frolicking lines,
Silly hats with goofy signs.
They twist and flip in sunny beams,
Like a village of wild dreams.

Frogs can leap and balloons float,
A squirrel in a bowler coat.
Windy giggles lift us high,
As balloons politely wave goodbye.

A kite with glitter in its tail,
Goes soaring past, what a scale!
Birds chime in with their own flair,
Joining in the joyous air.

With each new gust, the fun expands,
Unexpected ways across the lands.
So grab a friend, don't be shy,
Let's see just how far we can fly!

Celestial Strands Adrift

In the breeze, they dance and sway,
Like silly hats that love to play.
Twisting, turning, round they go,
Chasing clouds, putting on a show.

With every gust, they take a spin,
A graceful twirl, a cheeky grin.
They dip and dive without a care,
As if the sky was their fair share.

Emblems of Freedom and Flight

Oh, how they ripple, oh, how they cheer,
Escaping from the fence, never near.
They zigzag high, then plummet low,
Like kites with no strings, just going with flow.

Each twist a laugh, each flutter a joke,
Whispering tales, as if they spoke.
In their raucous dance, they find delight,
Painting the air, a comical sight.

The Artfulness of Breezy Adornments

They shimmy and shake in playful glee,
Inventing new moves, just to be free.
With sticky fingers, they cling to a branch,
In a scuffle and scramble, they start to prance.

A sudden gust, a twist of fate,
They soar through the sky, oh, what a date!
Adorned in laughter, a splendid parade,
Turning the mundane into a charade.

Spirited Flutters Under the Moon

At midnight's hour, they spin and twist,
Casting shadows, can't resist.
With moonlight sparkles, they daintily sway,
Giggling softly, come join the play.

These lively beings in the dark,
A whimsical show, a cheeky spark.
Under the stars, they skip and shout,
Celebrating freedom without a doubt.

Playful Whims of Air

Breezy dance on faun's delight,
A flutter here, a tickle there,
Socks on trees can't see the light,
As laughter spirals through the air.

Kites that try to snag the moon,
Swirling cookies, paper hats,
Chasing shadows, whistling tune,
Why do birds look like acrobats?

Floating leaves on tiny streams,
Acorns roll like round marbles,
Whimsical world of silly dreams,
While nature chuckles, she just troubles.

Caterpillars in a race,
Wobbling jelly, bumping foam,
A ladybug with silly grace,
Glad to join the chaos of home.

Ornamentation in Motion

Streamers swaying, oh so bright,
Laughter bubbles up with glee,
Silly hats take hourly flight,
While squirrels plot their big marquee.

Dandelions with puffball dreams,
Who knew they could tickle too?
A jester leaps, or so it seems,
As wind plays tag with random dew.

Twinkling chimes in playful spin,
Giggling flowers wave hello,
Each petal wants to join the din,
In tittering tales of ebb and flow.

Ribbons dance with carefree grace,
In a flurry of whims, they dip,
A marionette's merry chase,
Where all the sky takes a joyful trip.

Gentle Transformations of the Outdoors

Breezes bring a sweet surprise,
While tumbleweeds make silly turns,
Puffs of fluff bounce through the skies,
As mother nature giggles and learns.

Butterflies with ribbons bright,
Caterwauling 'round the trees,
In the chase of morning light,
Wisps of laughter tease the breeze.

Clouds play peek-a-boo in rays,
Spotting critters with a grin,
Walking trees in tiptoe frays,
Hiding secrets where they spin.

Every rustle tells a joke,
While petals prance on little feet,
As the wind begins to poke,
Nature's dance can't be beat!

Woven Whispers at Sundown

In twilight glow, fibers twist,
Laughter echoing 'neath the boughs,
Unruly seams are hard to resist,
As squirrels take their evening vows.

Shapes that wiggle, colors tease,
Stringy shadows flicker and flare,
Hopping crickets shoot the breeze,
Tickled by the softening air.

Frayed edges wink like old friends,
Knitting tales of fluttering fun,
Whispers join in jovial blends,
As the sky begins to run.

With every breeze, a riddle spins,
And so we dance 'til night declines,
In chuckles shared, adventure wins,
As the world unwinds its lines.

Velvet Ribbons Unfurled

In the park, a bow flew high,
Like a kite in the blue sky.
It wrapped around a squeaky dog,
Who chased it through the morning fog.

A lady's hat took off one day,
It danced and twirled, oh what a play!
The pigeons clucked, all in a row,
While children giggled at the show.

A swirling breeze, a fluttering skirt,
The ice cream man just spilled his slurt.
Cone hats now on a farmer's sheep,
They rolled and tumbled in a heap.

With laughter loud, the world spins bright,
In every gust, there's pure delight.
So let's all laugh and let it flow,
As ribbons wave and spirits glow.

Untethered Dreams

A pillow sailed across the street,
With nap-time clouds beneath its feet.
It flipped and flopped, then took a dive,
To land near Gus, who played jive.

A sudden breeze swept through the town,
Turning frowns to silly crowns.
With a whoosh, old hats took flight,
As squirrels cheered with pure delight.

Tea bags danced a jig within their pot,
Each dip and swirl, a silly plot.
The spoons took part in merry spins,
While laughter rang as joy begins.

In dreamland where the windy sways,
We float along in goofy ways.
So hold on tight to thoughts so free,
For funny winds bring glee, not glee.

Flicker of Forgotten Tales

Once a book sat on a shelf,
With dusty dreams, it sought itself.
A breeze blew through, it came alive,
And danced around like 'Twas a jive!

The pages flipped with giggles bright,
Each word revealed a quirky fright.
From dragons made of candy floss,
To pirates chasing after sauce.

Old ghosts in boots began to prance,
While tables joined in for a dance.
So here's to stories, wild and grand,
That flutter about at whimsy's hand.

In every gust, a tale will twirl,
Painting smiles in this wacky world.
With laughter ringing, we shall prevail,
In the flicker of forgotten tales.

Breezy Serenades

The flowers giggle in the breeze,
With petals flapping like grandpees.
A tulip slyly trips a bee,
Who buzzes back, "Oh, let me be!"

A choir of leaves begins to sing,
Each note flits lightly on soft wing.
The sun beams down, with silly rays,
As garden gnomes join in the plays.

A cloud rolls by in a fluffy hat,
It teases cats, who chase, then spat.
With every pounce and playful leap,
They tumble down, all in a heap.

So come and dance with nature's cheer,
With breezy tunes, we turn and steer.
In laughter's arms, the world won't fade,
As joy is found in every braide.

Playful Airborne Flourishes

In the sky they twist and turn,
Dancing high with flair to burn.
Whirling colors, lost in flight,
Chasing giggles, pure delight.

Gigantic bows on breezy prance,
Waving gently in a dance.
Tickling clouds with all their cheer,
Laughter echoes, loud and clear.

Around the trees, they make a fuss,
Twirling fast, each silly gust.
Who knew strings could have such fun?
Spinning tales 'til day is done.

They catch the sun, and then they gleam,
Each a tiny, silly dream.
Floating high, they mock the ground,
In their joy, we're all spellbound.

A Tangle of Dreams Amongst Starlight

Among the stars, they weave and play,
Spinning wishes far away.
A jumbled thread of hopes untied,
In the night, they take a ride.

Glittering beams in giddy loops,
Whirling high, as giggly troops.
Who created this funny show?
A cosmos filled with twists aglow.

With each gust, a dream escapes,
Floating high like silly shapes.
Starlit journeys, who can tell?
In the tangle, all is well.

And though they're lost, we watch and laugh,
Chasing tailwinds, goofy drafts.
In the sky, they play their game,
A frenzy of whimsy, wild and tame.

Ornate Echoes of the Past

Echoes whisper through the air,
Decorative spins, they have flair.
Olden days now flit and fly,
Nostalgia laughs, oh me, oh my!

Frilled and fanciful, they glide,
Ancient tales in light abide.
Winding history up above,
Silly tales wrapped tight with love.

Each little scroll has stories bright,
Whirling round in pure delight.
Forgotten colors, vibrant hue,
Cackles dance, as they renew.

With a chuckle, they will tease,
Rusty memories on the breeze.
In timeless pirouettes, they cheer,
Echoing joy through yesteryear.

The Freedom of Unraveled Yarns

Unraveled threads upon the ground,
Playfully scattered all around.
They tickle toes, then play tag,
Giggles burst as they all wag.

Tangles form like wild hairdos,
Laughter rising in bright hues.
They pirouette without a care,
Living free, dancing everywhere.

Knotted dreams turn into fun,
Each little twist beneath the sun.
In their chaos, joy unfolds,
Mischief spun in vibrant folds.

The strings set loose, they twine and tease,
Breezy shouts like playful bees.
Freedom found in every reel,
Unraveled joy, the greatest feel.

Gale-Kissed Fragments

A mad dash of color flits by,
Bright bits of joy that seem to fly.
Chasing the breeze, they leap and twirl,
Whispering secrets, as they swirl.

Tickled by laughter, the daisies sway,
Giggling petals join in the play.
The grass snickers with a tickle of cheer,
As nature dances—all here, no fear.

Bugs take a spin; it's a real hoedown,
With crunching leaves wearing a crown.
Wild winds weave mischief, crisp and spry,
As hats take flight and zoom on by.

Breezy jests flutter across the scene,
Nature's comedy, bold and keen.
With every gust, there's a chuckle anew,
In this festival where laughter grew.

Nature's Silken Brushes

Colors collide in a playful spree,
Nature's art with a twist of glee.
Brushes of foliage sweep left and right,
Creating a canvas, a comical sight.

Clouds drift lazily, plotting surprise,
With a wink and a grin, they dance in the skies.
Breezes toss giggles through flowers so bright,
Whisking away worries like feathers in flight.

The sun plays peek-a-boo, bright and bold,
Tickling the petals, both young and old.
A cacophony of sounds, the birds join in,
Celebrating life with a cheeky grin.

Each sway and shift becomes a delight,
As nature laughs deep into the night.
With splashes of crazy and quirks in tow,
The canvas of life continues to grow.

Odes to the Unseen

Lurking in shadows, who do we find?
Whispers and giggles, the mischief unlined.
Invisible dance, a raucous routine,
Painted by breezes, where none have been.

A polka-dotted spider spins threads of glee,
While ants stage a party, just wait and see.
The mushrooms are rumored to waltz on their own,
While the crickets resound with a musical tone.

Oh, the jests played upon the wind's back,
Echoes of laughter none can unpack.
The mysteries swirl, tickle and tease,
In the world of the unseen, where nonsense is key.

But look, there's a wisp in the twilight's glow,
Crafting its stories in a playful flow.
An ode to the silence of those who won't show,
In the heart of the wild, where giggles grow.

Flowing with the Wind

A dandelion puffs, a daring leap,
As laughter erupts from those who can't keep.
Whirls of petals trip in the skies,
Chasing each other with playful surprise.

The trees bend low, sharing a joke,
While squirrels team up and silliness stokes.
Fluffy clouds drift, plotting their scheme,
As shadows stretch out, embracing the dream.

With every gust, a new slapstick act,
Twisting and turning, never looked back.
The whims of the air tickle our senses,
As giggles with colors jump over fences.

Through laughter and light, the world takes a spin,
Embracing the wild, letting joy seep in.
Navigating the fun that will never rescind,
Floating, just floating, all thanks to the wind.

Ethereal Threads of Hope.

In a land where sunlight bounces,
And sparrows wear tiny trousers,
A thread of joy did twirl and spin,
Inviting all to join the din.

With silly hats and socks askew,
They danced beneath the sky so blue,
Each thread a wink, a laugh, a cheer,
As winds of jest would draw them near.

Whispers of Fluttering Threads

A breeze passed by with chuckles low,
As ribbons raced to steal the show,
They tangled, knotted, laughed out loud,
A colorful, chaotic crowd.

With every twist a new surprise,
They danced and giggled 'neath the skies,
In every flutter, joy conveyed,
And with each leap, new friends were made.

Dancing Fringes of Dusk

At twilight's door, the frayed ends sway,
Where shadows greet the end of day,
They jive around with silly grace,
Each twist and turn, a smiling face.

With whispers soft and muted glee,
The fringes jostle, wild and free,
As dusk approaches in a whirl,
They beckon on the evening's twirl.

Echoes in the Breeze.

In laughter's wake, the echoes sing,
As threads entwine in playful spring,
They sway like dancers, light and spry,
While giggles rise to greet the sky.

"Catch me if you can!" they tease,
With wiggles 'neath the gentle trees,
Each breath a promise, fun declared,
While breezes laughed, none ever scared.

Fringe of Dreams

Bouncing threads in playful cheer,
A jester's cap, so full of glee.
They twist and turn, no sense of fear,
A dance of fabric, wild and free.

They wave at clouds, salute the sun,
In jaunty moves, they prance and sway.
A party with no need for fun,
Just lively threads that love to play.

Caught in breezes, oh what a sight!
They tickle noses, tease the sky.
With flair they flaunt, oh what a flight,
These flapping pals, they never lie!

In dreams they roam, a funny crew,
Sipping laughter from an air-filled cup.
In every gust, a joyous view,
With exuberance, they bounce right up!

Fluttering Whispers

Whispers giggle, flapping high,
Like silly secrets on a breeze.
They tickle noses, pass on by,
Creating laughter with such ease.

Chasing after playful flights,
In a flirtatious breeze they tease.
A flutter here, then out of sights,
A game of hide and seek with leaves.

They dance like marionettes on strings,
With secrets shared, that no one knows.
In fancy patterns, laughter sings,
As whispers flutter and then doze.

Each spin a joke, each twirl a grin,
As whispers hide in softest breath.
They sprout wings where giggles begin,
Until their charm brings joy from death!

Dance of the Breezes

A jig is danced with airy glee,
When gusts come in, they stomp and sway.
With polka dots and stripes so free,
They whirl about till they decay.

Each tickle sends a ripple round,
As chuckles hide in breezy folds.
The breeze will wear the colors found,
In loose tuxedos, wild and bold.

Like silly clowns in circus hats,
They wobble, wiggle, laugh, and creak.
A carnival of wobbly spats,
With giggles bursting—what a peek!

Oh, how they flutter, dip, and dive,
With laughs that tickle, bold and sweet.
In breezy ballrooms, they survive,
The dance of air, forever neat!

Adrift in the Air

Floating ribbons, no fixed care,
They sail through skies, without a map.
A little breeze, a twist of flair,
In giggly gusts, they take their nap.

With playful twirls, they tease and chase,
Like puppies lost in softest dreams.
They bounce around, such lively grace,
In jovial moods, they want ice creams!

They surf on waves of gusty talk,
While daisies laugh at their delight.
In silly tumbles, they all walk,
Creating fun from sheer goodnight.

So here they dance, afloat, so grand,
These wayward whims in laughter's air.
In every flick, a touch of brand,
In breezy bliss, they've found their flair!

Currents of Color

A kite flew high, a sight to see,
With little kids shouting, "Look at me!"
Its tail swirled like spaghetti on a spree,
Chasing after clouds, wild and free.

A gust came strong, oh what a surprise,
It flipped and spun right before our eyes.
The neighbor's dog joined with furious cries,
As polka-dots danced in the bright blue skies.

With each tug and pull, it zigged and zagged,
Around the tree stump, oh how it bragged!
Laughing together, our hearts all wagged,
As color collided, and nobody lagged.

So let it roll on, let joy unwind,
Each thread's a giggle that twirls in the wind.
In the flurry of laughter, we all are aligned,
With dreams taking flight, let the fun never end!

Whirling Tales of the Sky

Once a balloon decided to play,
It flicked and flapped, then floated away.
Telling tales to birds, oh what a display,
Of avocado pickle pies coming our way!

A squirrel looked up, with eyes open wide,
As the balloon twirled with whimsical pride.
Its string got caught—oh what a ride!
That fruity balloon's wildly untried!

A windy twist left it spinning around,
Like a jolly old elf in a merry-go-round.
With giggles and cheers, friends gathered 'round,
To catch the balloon before it was drowned.

So here in the park, we laugh and we cheer,
For the skies are our stage, and we've nothing to fear.
With whirling old tales and laughter sincere,
The balloons in the sky always bring joy near!

The Graceful Flight

A feather drifted, soft on the breeze,
It tickled the nose of a grand old cheese.
As the mice chimed in, "Oh, what a tease!"
They danced with the swans, all aiming to please.

Up floated a paper, drawn with a smile,
It glided along with carefree style.
But oh, what a sight! With each little mile,
It ended up stuck in a tree for a while.

Then down came the wind, with a mischievous flair,
Tugging and pulling, it tossed with great care.
Our laughter erupted, wild in the air,
As the paper took flight, shedding worry and despair.

A floating parade, with grace so absurd,
Each twist and each turn made the moment superb.
And though we're all grounded, our spirits all stirred,
With each feathered flight, we're forever assured!

Woven Wonders Above

In the sky's loom, colors tease and entwine,
A tapestry woven, both silly and fine.
With giggles galore, patterns align,
As clouds play hopscotch, like children divine.

Oh, what a comical dance in the air,
A kite with polka-dots, and a rainbow to share.
Caught in a riddle, twirling without care,
Even the sun seems to stop and stare!

With whispers of laughter that travel the way,
We ride on the breezes, with no need to pay.
Each twist, every turn, brightened our day,
In delight of the wonders that ever convey.

So here's to the colors that brighten our skies,
With joy in the chase, and sparkles in eyes.
As we laugh at the patterns that dance and arise,
In the woven tales above, our imaginations fly!

Melody of the Fluttering Fringe

Little strands dance in the breeze,
Whirling like they're in a tease.
Chasing shadows, they sway and spin,
Laughing at the trouble they're in.

A feathery jig with no real clue,
Bouncing like they're on a pogo too.
They trip on air and take a bow,
Oh my, what chaos! Take a count now!

Bright threads sillier than a clown's grand hat,
Hitching rides on a curious cat.
One tried to tango with a passing bee,
But got too dizzy—oh, not so free!

A concert of colors swings their way,
Adding laughter to a sunny day.
Together they march, a silly brigade,
Who knew fringe had such funny parades?

Colourful Signatures in Motion

In vibrant strokes, they write their tale,
Swinging wildly, like a ship with a sail.
Every flap a giggle, every spin a cheer,
They paint the sky—hi, look over here!

With knots and loops, they loop-de-loop,
Creating a circus, a giggling troupe.
One pink strand wore polka dots bold,
While another told stories of mischief untold.

Trying to mingle, they tangle in knots,
Spinning tales about what they are not.
A green one declared itself a grand king,
But tripped on a breeze—oh, the chaos it brings!

A waltz with the clouds, oh what a sight,
They twist and they spin, they jump with delight.
With each swish, they sketch a new line,
Making our world feel so funny and fine!

Floating Fables Woven in Time

They drift through the air, these stories untold,
Chasing the laughter, so foolishly bold.
A swirl of hues, a jolly parade,
Weaving adventures in every charade.

One tale of a thread that got lost in the puff,
Claiming it's tough, but it's really just fluff.
It swung on a breeze, oh what a ride,
A fable of fun where the giggles abide.

With each little flip, a new story's begun,
Juggling chaos, oh, what silly fun!
They argue and laugh, these threads in a race,
Creating a ruckus in a fanciful space.

As night draws near, they whisper and share,
Of silly mishaps and whimsical flair.
Floating through time, they craft and they cheer,
Fables of laughter for all to revere!

The Breath of Ornate Threads

Winds whisper secrets, lace takes flight,
Threads of mischief under starlight.
Spinning like tops, they twirl with glee,
What's that line? It's just me being free!

Juggling emotions, they flounder and flop,
One grabbed a leaf, oh dear, what a stop!
Entwined in a swirl, they dance and they play,
Life's a grand jest, come join the ballet!

Each weave a chuckle, each knot a laugh,
Bouncing around on a whimsical path.
They play silly games, but never complain,
Sailing through joy like a kid in the rain.

A blend of the foolish, a patchwork of cheer,
In this tapestry, all troubles disappear.
Threads of the night, let's celebrate you,
For bringing us smiles, oh so bright and true!

The Chorus of Ornate Lines

In the garden, strings of grace,
Flapping wildly, a curious race,
Each bead of laughter, a twist and twirl,
Fashion statements, like a colorful whirl.

Breezy banter, they sashay and sway,
Whispering jokes as they dance away,
A garden party with giggles galore,
Connect the threads, let the laughter soar.

With the sun gleaming, they plot and scheme,
A conga line of a funny dream,
In the sunlight, they chatter and tease,
Waving hello to the teasing breeze.

Jumps and jigs in a playful spree,
Nature's confetti, wild and free,
Fanciful threads in a vibrant show,
A chorus of colors, stealing the glow.

Celestial Flutters and Whispers

Up in the sky, a comedy flight,
Feathers and fluff taking off in delight,
Making circles with glorious flair,
Painted in laughter, floating in air.

They tickle clouds, in a jolly spree,
Whirling round, oh what a sight to see,
Giggles escaping like bubbles of fun,
Chasing the moon till the day is done.

Serenading stars with a whimsical tune,
Bouncing rays light up the afternoon,
With every flutter, a chuckle they share,
Kites of humor dancing with care.

Each twirl and twist, a giggly closure,
Knotted laughter in cosmic exposure,
With every whisper, the skies enthrall,
A quilt of joy, over all.

Currents of Adorned Reality

In the marketplace, a vibrant spree,
Colors colliding with glee,
Shimmering baubles, swapping tales,
Sailing time on bouncy trails.

Chimes and clangs, a raucous glee,
Handcrafted wonders on display to see,
A carousel of odd, shaped delight,
Turning heads with a pop and a bite.

Threaded wonders in rows so bright,
Jesting in fabric, a colorful sight,
As laughter drips from every seam,
Reality weaves into a funny dream.

Amidst the hustle, they spin and weave,
Jokes and fabric, never to leave,
In joyous contrasts, they switch and sway,
Dress up the dull, in a colorful play.

The Dance of the Subtle Strands

In the twilight, they start to prance,
Whirling brightly in a merry dance,
Whisking away all the woes, you see,
Strands of joy, wild and free.

Cascading ribbons in playful twine,
Wiggling along a sparkling line,
Hearts afloat on a playful breeze,
Their silly antics sure to please.

In moonlit hues, the laughter grows,
Where each flicker of light gently glows,
Threads of mirth woven with care,
A tapestry of giggles in the air.

Dancing shadows bring stories of cheer,
Cackles echoing, sweet and near,
In the dance of strands, all come alive,
Where the humor of life will always thrive.

Epic Flutters of Fate

In a meadow where breezes play,
Socks dance wildly, what a display!
The cows are chuckling, grass in their teeth,
While butterflies tease the old oak beneath.

A hat took flight on a gusty spree,
Chasing a squirrel up a tall pine tree.
The cat watched closely, her tail in a twist,
Wondering why it's all come to this!

A kite and a chicken in comical chase,
Flap and squawk without a trace.
Laughter erupts as the sun starts to dip,
A pancake flips, what a funny trip!

As daylight fades, the giggles fuse,
With whispers of night, they'll all diffuse.
The epic flutters, from far and wide,
Are tales of adventure and laughter inside.

Flowing Strands of Memory

Silly socks tangled on the line,
Twirling around, oh, how they shine!
Grandma's stories of dancing shoes,
And how she once lost her left to the blues.

Knots of laughter in the fading light,
With grandpa's mustache taking flight!
The dog thinks it's all a great game,
Chasing the memories like they're to blame.

A summer breeze and a raucous laugh,
As kids spin in circles, making a gaff.
The cat joins in with an unplanned leap,
Haunting their dreams while they sleep.

Through flowing strands of joy so bright,
Shadows dance in the soft moonlight.
Memory flutters, a cheerful kerfuffle,
In the heart, they all happily shuffle!

Cascading Ribbons of Nostalgia

Ribbons roll down the birthday lane,
Tangled and twisted but never in vain.
Balloons are plotting a funny prank,
While the cake's sitting pretty, with frosting rank.

A grand celebration that went a bit wrong,
The piñata fell flat, oh, what a song!
Children erupted in giggles and glee,
As candy exploded, a sugary spree.

Confetti rains down like a shimmering laugh,
Splat on the noses—a photographic gaffe!
With sticky fingers and joyous delight,
They'll remember this chaos long into the night.

In cascading colors, the past sways and bends,
Every tangle brings laughter, the best of friends.
As dusk settles down, and the stars peek through,
Nostalgia spins tales, forever anew.

Hummingbird's Silken Touch

A tiny bird zips past my head,
With a whirr and a chuckle, it quickly fled.
It stole my drink, can you even believe?
And left me here wondering, 'How does it deceive?'

Fluffing its feathers like a royal parade,
It flutters and pirouettes, oh, what a charade!
While bees stack their buzz like a comical tune,
The flowers are giggling beneath the bright moon.

With skills of a gymnast, it dances and plays,
Hovering near to steal all the praise.
Then off to a petal, it whips with a grin,
A caper of mischief, just look at it spin!

Hummingbird's magic, a feathered delight,
Bringing laughter together, oh, what a sight!
In silken embrace, the world starts to bloom,
With whispers of joy that break through the gloom.

Whirling Silks of Autumn

Leaves in a dance, twirling bright,
Chasing each other, what a sight!
A squirrel winks, thinks it's a game,
As he rolls back, feels no shame.

Pumpkins in hats, twirled on their heads,
Giggling with glee, in cozy beds.
Frolicking vines join the cheer,
Spinning around, they disappear!

Whirlwinds laugh with playful grace,
As branches sway, we join the race.
Funny how nature takes its spin,
Reminder that joy's where we begin!

Autumn's parade keeps us in glee,
A swirling fest, so wild and free.
In this bright season, let's all parade,
With laughter and fun, the memories made.

Swaying Embellishments Above

A bell ornament dangles on high,
Looking like it's ready to fly.
With each gust, it clinks and sways,
A chirpy tune, in comical ways.

The clouds are fluff, cotton-candy dreams,
Dodging sunlight, bursting at seams.
Funny shades in delight they display,
Like toddlers in costumes, at play all day.

Balloons drift by, chasing the breeze,
Tugging at strings like a band of bees.
Each pop and puff brings giggles galore,
As they sail and sway, always wanting more!

Above us swirls a colorful fest,
Nature's own joke, we must confess.
Swaying embellishments, wild and bright,
Make us chuckle, pure sheer delight.

Veils of Morning Light

Morning whispers, wrapped in cheer,
A laugh escapes—a whoops! Oh dear!
Sunbeams play peek-a-boo in delight,
Casting veils that dance, oh so light!

Bugs in bow ties, buzzing about,
Trying to figure this laughter route.
With breakfast spills, and crumbs a-fly,
Even the toast seems to wave hi!

Puppies chase rays, dashing so fast,
Shaking their tails, a joyful blast.
With dashes and zigzags that brighten our day,
In the morn's gentle sparkle, they giggle and play.

Veils of light twinkle all 'round,
Nature's parade, such joy abound.
In the early sun's warm embrace,
Morning's laughter, the best kind of grace.

Songs of the Cascading Fringe

Ribbons of color, flapping with glee,
Dance like a choir, wild and free.
Oversized hats jump on the stage,
Twirling and swaying, free of cage.

Fringes that giggle, wiggling bright,
A playful sonata, pure delight.
Swinging and jumping, what a wild spree,
Who knew fabrics could be so carefree?

Jesters in patterns, colors collide,
Spinning and swaying, none can hide.
As laughter erupts, guiding the show,
The audience chuckles, go with the flow!

Cascading tunes give joy a spin,
Nature's own party, where to begin?
In this grand opera of fun to engage,
With songs of fringe, we all take the stage!

Lofty Embers of the Sky

In the rafters, kites take flight,
With squeaks and giggles, oh what a sight!
They whirl and twirl, dramatic flair,
While folks below just stop and stare.

Balloons go pop, the laughter swells,
As pigeons plot their funny spells.
A rainbow wig on a sunlit cat,
Chasing shadows, what's up with that?

Juggling squirrels on a high-wire beam,
Cotton candy clouds in a silly dream.
Blown away with each gusty gust,
Oh, how we laugh, oh how we trust!

With every breeze, a new delight,
A silly dance 'neath starry light.
So here we bask in joy so spry,
With lofty embers shooting high!

Breeze-Caught Dreams

In the park, a kite on a spree,
Chasing the wind like it's set free.
It dips and dives, with a honk or two,
While picnics scatter with a funny boo!

Ice cream cones fly like rocket ships,
As ducks leap out with quacking slips.
A flip-flop lands on a tree so bold,
And leaves the onlookers laughing, uncontrolled.

Sun hats dance, oh what a scene,
Twisting about like a goofy machine.
Laughter echoes through every lane,
As squirrels practice their stand-up gain.

A breeze catches jokes spun in the air,
Floating like whispers without a care.
With every gust, the giggles gleam,
In this world where all is a dream.

Unruly Streams of Light

Light beams bouncing, oh what a sight,
Like cats on skates in the warm sunlight.
Chasing shadows beneath the trees,
They leap and pounce like a playful sneeze.

A disco ball spins in the park's blue,
While fireflies flash like they own the view.
The sunwaves dance like they're in a race,
A silly twist in this joyous space.

Whimsical whispers in the golden hour,
Tickle the flowers, oh what a power!
Their petals shake, giggle and sway,
A laughter bridge to the end of the day.

From dawn's first glimpse to twilight's glow,
Laughter rolls, with a vibrant flow.
In unruly streams, we float so bright,
In this comic chase of pure delight.

Vibrant Whispers of Change

Breezes bring news from afar,
Of dancing leaves and a sweeping star.
A hat takes flight, tumbling bold,
With secrets of laughter it has told.

Socks mismatched walk a charming route,
While squirrels mime in a fleece-lined suit.
A breeze blows in, and what do we see?
A squirrel in sunglasses, how funny is he!

Bubbles rise, swaying in glee,
Chasing the flutter of bees you can see.
Each pop and giggle, a joyful refrain,
As vibrant whispers beg us to remain.

In the chaos of nature, we find our way,
With smiles that dance and hearts that play.
With every gust, like a gentle nudge,
We embrace the change, laugh, and budge.

Wandering Fringes

Fringes dance in a flurry,
Caught in a playful hurry.
Twirling like a happy bee,
Peeking at the world so free.

Tickled by the breeze's kiss,
They laugh at a moment's bliss.
Swinging high and swinging low,
Oh, where will the next wind blow?

Chasing clouds, they do the jig,
In a twirl, they'd spin so big.
A comedy of fluttering flair,
Hiding secrets in the air.

With colors bright and hearts so bold,
Every twist a tale retold.
These silly strands know how to play,
Making each dull moment sway.

Cascading Colors

Colors tumble, bright and loud,
Beneath the sky, they feel so proud.
A splash here, a dash there,
A rainbow's giggle in the air.

They leap from trees, they swirl around,
Painting laughter on the ground.
In a game of peek-a-boo,
They laugh at clouds, it's true, it's true!

With every gust, they wave and sway,
Irritating the dog at play!
Whimsical chatter fills the scene,
In a swirl of colors, oh so keen.

A rooster's call, a sudden trip,
The party frays at edges' grip.
But still, they twirl with sheer delight,
Even the sun is grinning bright.

The Whimsy of Movement

Whimsical jumps, a jig so spry,
Skirted edges waving high.
In the breeze, they find their song,
Dancing where the funny belongs.

A gust of wind, a wild spin,
Creating chaos with a grin.
Onward in a tumble, they dash,
Leaving laughter in their flash.

They tease the passerby with flair,
Tickling noses, ruffling hair.
Every flap, a giggle released,
In movement's grip, they are the least.

From clumsy flips to merry loops,
Their antics charm and woo the troops.
In fields of glee, they whirl away,
A jesting ballet, come what may.

Swaying Moments of Grace

Moments sway, like kids at play,
In a game of hop and sway.
One misstep and then they fall,
Crafting laughter, that's their call.

Each gentle breeze a little joke,
Tickling the world, like a thoughtful poke.
As they sway, they seem to play,
Drawing chuckles from the day.

They wiggle, flutter, arch, and dive,
In their silly dance, they thrive.
A ribbon caught in laughter's tide,
With every gust, fun multiplies.

So here's to moments filled with glee,
Where joy and grace are wild and free.
With every twist, a giggle's prize,
A swirling laugh beneath the skies.

Overhead Dreams in Motion

Balloons escape with glee,
Like squirrels on caffeine,
Chasing the clouds, they sway,
In the most ridiculous way.

Sun hats dance to a tune,
Giggling beneath the moon,
Kites perform a silly show,
What a sight, don't you know?

Straws in drinks take to flight,
Twisting left and right,
Bouncy castles flap alive,
Jokes on kids, who won't survive!

Pies on windowsills tease,
Hoping bees don't seize,
Chaos reigns in the air,
As laughter fills everywhere.

Specters of Suspended Finesse

Ghostly ribbons float so high,
Dancing fools in the sky,
They twirl with such flair,
Who needs a chair?

Invisible strings hold tight,
As cats chase shadows at night,
Whiskers twitch, then they pounce,
A feline circus, they prance.

Socks left on the line,
Unsuited for sunshine,
They wave and they cheer,
A laundry-day frontier!

Leaves pretend to take flight,
As squirrels skills ignite,
Cartwheeling across the grass,
Nature's jester, oh alas!

Fluttering Hues in the Open Sky

Crayons lost their little minds,
In a spoonful of sunshine finds,
Colorful antics on display,
A joyful, messy array.

Fluffy clouds join the fun,
Making faces, one by one,
They taunt and tease like kin,
On the breeze, let's begin!

Cupcakes with sprinkles on top,
Whisking 'round, they won't stop,
Chasing sprightly butterflies,
With icing dreams in their eyes.

Streamers in playful flutters,
As the sausage dog stutters,
Dances that no one can see,
Life's a party, let it be!

Eloquent Shifts in the Breeze

Breezy whispers tickle round,
As the chubby cats astound,
Rolling over just for fun,
Chasing shadows, everyone!

Umbrellas take a spin,
Like they're in a shaky din,
Mad capers in the square,
As if they just don't care!

Pillow fights up in the air,
Soft as whispers, light as hair,
Feathers drift on ethereal streams,
Reality blends with silly dreams.

Twirl of skirts and laughter bright,
Making even the dull feel light,
In this moment of delight,
Every cheeky whim takes flight!